D1266722

12 REASONS TO LOVE
SOCCER

by Brian Trusdell

STORY LIBRARY

www.12StoryLibrary.com

12-Story Library is an imprint of Bookstaves and Press Room Editions

Produced for 12-Story Library by Red Line Editorial

Photographs ©: Matthew Visinsky/Icon Sportswire/AP Images, cover, 1; John Dorton/Shutterstock Images, 4; Bain News Service/George Grantham Bain Collection/Library of Congress, 5; ChameleonsEye/Shutterstock Images, 6; Denis Linine/Shutterstock Images, 7; Pal2iyawit/Shutterstock Images, 8; Sydney Low/Cal Sports Media/AP Images, 9; barbsimages/Shutterstock Images, 10; Ververidis Vasilis/Shutterstock Images, 11; Marcos Mesa Sam Wordley/Shutterstock Images, 12; Ted S. Warren/AP Images, 13; Lao Qiang Xa/Imaginechina/AP Images, 14, 29; AP Images, 15, 18; AGIF/Shutterstock Images, 16; Kathleen Hinkel/Icon Sportswire/AP Images, 17; Mark J. Terrill/AP Images, 19, 28; Jonathan Hayward/The Canadian Press/AP Images, 20; Antonio Scorza/Shutterstock Images, 21; Matt Dunham/AP Images, 22; Soutello/AGIF/Rex Features/AP Images, 23; A.Ricardo/Shutterstock Images, 24; Andy Clayton-King/AP Images, 25; Lacy Atkins/The San Francisco Examiner/AP Images, 27

Library of Congress Cataloging-in-Publication Data
Names: Trusdell, Brian, author.
Title: 12 reasons to love soccer / by Brian Trusdell.
Other titles: Twelve reasons to love soccer
Description: Mankato, Minnesota : 12 Story Library, 2018. | Series: Sports
    report | Includes bibliographical references and index. | Audience: Grade
    4 to 6.
Identifiers: LCCN 2016047349 (print) | LCCN 2016052599 (ebook) | ISBN
    9781632354303 (hardcover : alk. paper) | ISBN 9781632354990 (pbk. : alk.
    paper) | ISBN 9781621435518 (hosted e-book)
Subjects: LCSH: Soccer--Juvenile literature.
Classification: LCC GV943.25 .T78 2018 (print) | LCC GV943.25 (ebook) | DDC
    796.334--dc23
LC record available at https://lccn.loc.gov/2016047349

Printed in China
022017

Access free, up-to-date content on this topic plus a full digital version of this book. Scan the QR code on page 31 or use your school's login at 12StoryLibrary.com.

Table of Contents

Soccer Is Simple

Soccer has been called "the Beautiful Game." It has also been called "the Simplest Game." It gets these nicknames because it has such a simple idea: players must kick a ball into a goal. Because soccer is a simple game, it doesn't need fancy equipment.

Actually, players don't even need a ball. Brazilian superstar Pelé grew up very poor in Brazil. He played with a sock stuffed with rags or newspaper. He became one of the greatest players in history.

There aren't many rules, or laws, in soccer. An English group called the Football Association wrote some of the earliest laws more than 150 years ago. The four oldest laws are about the field, the ball, the number of players, and the equipment.

The most basic law is that field players are not allowed to touch

No one needs helmets or special sticks to play soccer.

17

Number of laws in soccer.

- Soccer is a simple game.
- The first laws were written more than 150 years ago.
- The simplest rule is that players can't use their hands, except for the goalkeeper.

the ball with their hands. Only the goalkeeper can do that. Goalkeepers can use their hands in the penalty area around the goal. Soccer's easy rules help make it the most popular sport in the world.

RULE CHANGES

The International Football Association Board (IFAB) meets every year to review the rules. Eight people are on the board. One member comes from each of the original countries in the Football Association. The countries are England, Scotland, Wales, and Northern Ireland. Four more people come from the Fédération Internationale de Football Association (FIFA). FIFA is the organization that oversees soccer worldwide.

An English association football team from 1912

It's Played Almost Everywhere

Soccer is a worldwide sport. It's played in parks across the United States. It's played on fields in African villages. It's played in the streets of Brazilian cities. Soccer is one of the most popular sports in the world. More than 24 million people play soccer in the United States alone.

Soccer is called football in many places across the globe. In particular, it's sometimes called association football. This traces back to the Football Association organization that first wrote the modern laws. They called their sport association football to tell it apart from rugby football. Rugby is an old sport that's like soccer, but players may use their hands.

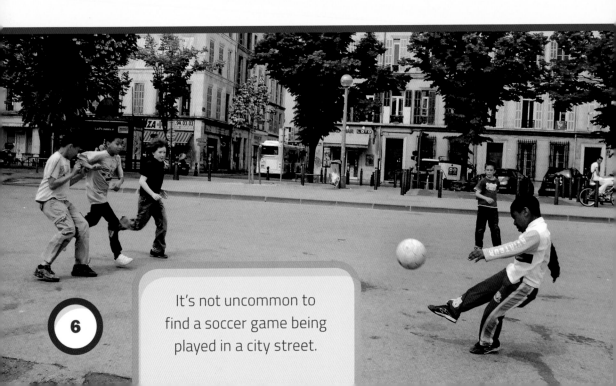

It's not uncommon to find a soccer game being played in a city street.

THE CHRISTMAS GAME

One of the oddest places for a soccer game to occur was on a World War I (1914–1918) battlefield. On Christmas Day in 1914, the German and British troops stopped fighting each other. The soldiers came out of their trenches and played soccer together.

Soccer is a British word. The *soc* in *soccer* comes from the word *association*. In England at the time, it was common to shorten words and add *er* to them.

Whatever it's called, soccer is popular around the world. FIFA has 211 member countries. By comparison, only 193 countries belong to the United Nations. The United Nations is an organization of countries that work together for peace. FIFA is sometimes called the United Nations of Football.

270 million
Number of people who play organized soccer around the world.

- Soccer can be played nearly anywhere in the world.
- Soccer was originally called association football.
- More nations belong to FIFA than to the United Nations.

FIFA governs the sport all over the world.

FIFA®

For the Game. For the World.

FIFA®

MY GAME IS FAIR PLAY

Soccer Has Many Forms

Soccer players and fans know the basic rules of the sport: It has 11 players. It's played on a large field. The game lasts 90 minutes. It's divided into two halves.

But some people don't know there are many other forms of soccer. Futsal is played indoors. The field is the size of a basketball court. It's also called five-a-side. Only five players are on each team.

Indoor soccer is another version of the sport. In the United States, there are professional indoor soccer leagues. It's played on artificial turf over a hockey rink. Each team has six players. The games last up to 60 minutes. They are divided into four

Futsal brings the excitement of soccer indoors.

Practice drills feature new twists on soccer in order to build new skills.

periods. It's a fast sport. The ball can bounce off the walls.

There's also beach soccer. That's played on sand. It has five players on each team. FIFA has official rules for beach soccer as well as futsal.

Teams can play several types of games during practice. In one-touch, players gather in a circle and can only touch the ball once. Some teams practice with small-sided games. These are played on smaller fields with fewer players.

There's also soccer tennis. Just as it sounds, it combines soccer with tennis. Players kick a ball over a net. They can also head it over. That means hitting the ball with their

head. A net can be something as simple as rope strung between two chairs. The possibilities are endless for different ways to play soccer.

3

Number of 12-minute periods in a beach soccer game.

- There are many versions of soccer.
- FIFA has rules for futsal and beach soccer.
- Soccer practice sometimes includes small-sided games and one-touch.
- Soccer tennis uses a net.

The Action Never Stops

A soccer game is always moving. Players constantly run from one side of the field to the other. They must find ways to catch their breath during the action. Soccer players must be fit. They need stamina to keep up with the action.

At the professional level, the game is almost nonstop for the entire 90 minutes. There are no timeouts.

In soccer, the game keeps moving, and so do the players.

30

Seconds referees often add to the game to make up for goal celebrations.

- Soccer action hardly ever stops.
- When play does stop, it restarts quickly.
- The running clock never stops.

Play stops in only a few cases. It stops when the ball goes out of bounds. The referee can also stop play for a number of reasons. One reason might be a foul. A foul is called when the referee thinks a player did something unfair. Another reason is when a player is injured.

If play stops, it restarts quickly. Depending on why the game

YELLOW AND RED CARDS

When a player commits a serious foul, the referee shows a yellow piece of cardboard or plastic. This is called a yellow card. Two yellow cards in a game result in a red card. That means the player is kicked out of the game.

stopped, there are different ways to kick or throw the ball back into play.

One thing that never stops is the clock. It constantly ticks away. It's called a running clock. Referees keep track of how often the ball isn't in play during the game. This may include time teams take to celebrate after a goal. Referees can then add time at the end of each half to make up for lost action.

A player reacts to receiving a yellow card after a serious foul.

5

Fans Are Passionate about Soccer

Soccer fans are known to stand for entire games. They sing. They chant. They paint their faces. They light flares. They wave flags and hold up tifos. A tifo is a special display during a game.

Many teams have fan clubs. They wear the team colors. Some wear funny hats. Many fan clubs support national teams. These teams play in international tournaments, such as the Olympics and FIFA World Cup. The Tartan Army follows

THINK ABOUT IT

Why do you think fans are so passionate about soccer? What are the positive effects of fans' passion? What are the negative effects?

Scotland's team. The US team has the American Outlaws and Sam's Army. The American Outlaws fan club has more than 30,000 members in 175 chapters.

Tifo displays show fans' support on a huge scale.

Mascots such as Timber Joey can fire up the crowd.

Whole countries have been known to shut down during soccer games. Many businesses close so people can watch a game. Only restaurants stay open for fans to gather.

Some fans are just as excited about their local teams as they are about national teams. They travel far to watch their teams play.

Many teams use mascots to get fans more excited. A mascot is a character or thing that symbolizes a team. Fans cheer for the live eagle that soars over the Benfica team's stadium. Fans also go wild for Timber Joey. He's the Portland Timbers lumberjack. He wears a hard hat and cuts a log with a chainsaw after each goal.

196,838
Americans who bought tickets to watch Team USA in the 2014 men's World Cup games in Brazil.

- Soccer fans are passionate about their teams.
- Many national teams have fan clubs.
- Fans enjoy team mascots.

The Game Has a Long History

Games like soccer were played centuries ago. The Chinese had a game called Tsu' Chu or *cuju*. It may have been played more than 3,000 years ago. Around 600 CE, the Japanese created a game called Kemari. Both of these ancient games involved kicking something round.

Soccer-like games were also played in ancient Mediterranean cultures. The Greek game was called *episkyros*. It may have been played around 2000 BCE. Romans played *harpastum* around 500 BCE. It was loosely based on episkyros. Later, people from Florence, Italy, invented *calcio* in the 1500s. Italians still use the word *calcio* for soccer.

Modern soccer developed over many centuries in England. The sport was popular but also violent. It was often banned. But people kept playing it.

In 1869, two universities in the United States played a game using the Football Association rules of 1863. It's considered the first college soccer match. The game played that day is also considered an early

Players in China reenact the ancient game of cuju.

Uruguay beat Argentina in the first World Cup in 1930.

version of American football. Modern American football is a blend of soccer and rugby.

FIFA was founded in 1904. The first FIFA World Cup was played with just men's teams in 1930. The men's World Cup has grown from 13 teams in 1930 to 32 teams today. The Women's World Cup was first held in 1991.

THINK ABOUT IT

American football traces back to soccer. What similarities do you still see today in the two sports? What differences do you see?

1314

Year King Edward II banned soccer in England because it was too violent.

- Ancient people played games like soccer.
- The modern game of soccer is more than 150 years old.
- FIFA was founded in 1904.

15

Soccer Stars Are Known Worldwide

Every sport has its superstars. Soccer is loved worldwide, and so are its superstars.

Lionel Messi was born in Argentina. He's a hero there. But he's also a hero to fans of FC Barcelona in Spain, where he plays. Messi has won eight Spanish league championships with Barcelona. He's also won four Union of European Football Associations (UEFA) Champions League titles. UEFA oversees soccer in Europe.

With Argentina's national team, Messi won a FIFA Under-20

Of all the soccer stars in the world, Messi may be the greatest.

World Cup. He also led Argentina to an Olympic gold medal in 2008. He makes many millions in salary and endorsement deals.

Another high-paid soccer star is Cristiano Ronaldo. He's from Portugal. He plays for Real Madrid, another team in the Spanish league. When Messi's and Ronaldo's teams play each other, the game is called El Clásico. More than 400 million people worldwide watch the game.

Some US stars are known around the world, too. Many people know Abby Wambach is one of the best players to ever come from the United States. She led the United States to two Olympic gold medals. She's also won a World Cup championship. Wambach scored 184 goals in

77
Goals Abby Wambach has scored with her head.

- Soccer stars are famous all over the world.
- Lionel Messi and Cristiano Ronaldo are soccer superstars.
- More people watch Messi and Ronaldo in "El Clásico" than the Super Bowl.
- Abby Wambach is famous as one of the best US players of all time.

international matches. That's more than any other soccer player, male or female. In a 2004 match against Ireland, she scored five goals. She's especially known for heading the ball.

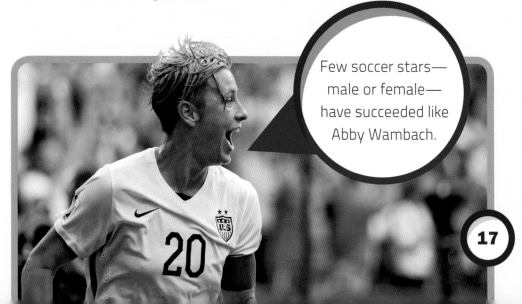

Few soccer stars— male or female— have succeeded like Abby Wambach.

Legends Have Shaped the Sport

Soccer stars of today are compared to the heroes of the past. Pelé led Brazil to three World Cup crowns. He won in 1958, 1962, and 1970. He is the only player to win three cups.

Diego Maradona is another soccer legend. He led Argentina to the 1986 World Cup title. Another star is Eusébio. He was called the Black Panther. He played for Portugal. He scored nine goals at the 1966 World Cup.

Mia Hamm is a legend who helped launch US women's soccer. Between 1991 and 2004, she led the United States to two Olympic gold medals and two World Cups. Her 158 international goals were once a world

No player has more World Cup wins than Pelé.

13

Goals scored by Just Fontaine in 1958, which still stand as the most in a single World Cup.

- Soccer's past includes many legendary players.
- Pelé and Maradona are some of the biggest stars in soccer history.
- Mia Hamm was a pioneer in women's soccer.

MARADONA'S TWO GOALS

In the 1986 World Cup Final, Diego Maradona scored two famous goals. On the first, he punched the ball with his hand. The referee didn't notice the foul. Maradona later said the ball was guided into the net by the "hand of God." Four minutes after that goal, he dribbled down half the field and past five defenders to score again.

record for men and women. Her former teammate Abby Wambach broke that record in 2013.

Some players become legends for a single moment. Joe Gaetjens scored only one goal in the 1950 World Cup. But it gave the United States a surprise win over England. The victory is one of the greatest upsets in World Cup history.

Mia Hamm inspired a generation of girls and women to play soccer.

19

Famous Teams Make the Game Great

Around the world, soccer fans are easy to spot. They walk the streets wearing jerseys, T-shirts, and hats of their favorite teams. They follow their teams' social media accounts.

Real Madrid and FC Barcelona are two of the most famous teams. Approximately 100 million fans follow each team on social media. The teams' jerseys are some of the most popular for sale. Of course, it helps that the teams have stars such as Messi and Ronaldo.

England has several famous teams as well. Manchester United and Chelsea may be the most popular. Manchester City, Arsenal, and Liverpool also are well known around the world.

The US women's team has earned a huge following after winning World Cups and gold medals.

The US women's team has millions of fans after

dominating international play for years. In 2015, 26.7 million people watched Team USA beat Japan in the World Cup final. It was the biggest audience for any US soccer match, men's or women's. After the win, team shirts and jerseys sold out overnight at many sporting goods stores.

In fact, jerseys are a major part of what makes teams popular around the world. The yellow and green jersey of the Brazilian national team is often seen on the streets of Rio de Janeiro. But it can also be seen on the streets of Tokyo. Brazil's jersey isn't the only one that stands out. Many other teams' jerseys can be recognized instantly. Soccer fans know Juventus's black and white stripes. FC Barcelona has famous blue and red stripes.

115 million
Number of followers FC Barcelona had on Facebook and Twitter in 2016.

- Soccer teams have strong followings.
- Real Madrid and FC Barcelona are famous.
- The US women's team draws huge television audiences.
- Jerseys are part of a team's popularity.

THINK ABOUT IT

Many soccer teams have fans all over the world. What role do you think the Internet and social media play in their popularity?

10 Soccer Has Many Championships

Because soccer is played across the world, there are many champions. There are different tournaments for men, women, youth, clubs, and national teams. All the championships make for fascinating games worldwide.

Many countries have their own championship. Professional and amateur clubs compete in knockout tournaments. Other champions are crowned through league play. Teams in Britain play for the Premier League title. Spanish clubs try for the La Liga championship.

Teams that win their countries' championships move on to the next level. Most continents have their own champions league. This is where continent champions are crowned. In Europe, teams compete for the UEFA Champions League title. In North America, teams play in the Confederation of North, Central America and Caribbean Association Football (CONCACAF).

Leicester City took home the Premier League championship in 2016.

FIFA organizes many international tournaments, including Olympic soccer.

The organization runs the Gold Cup and CONCACAF Champions League tournaments.

The best of the best play in global tournaments. FIFA oversees many worldwide tournaments. The FIFA World Cup is played every four years. It's for national teams. The men's and women's teams have their own tournaments.

FIFA has other tournaments as well. There's a championship for teams with players under 17 years old. This is called the U-17 World Cup. The U-20 World Cup features players under 20. Just as with the World Cup, men and women have their own tournaments for these age groups.

FIFA also organizes soccer for the Olympics and Youth Olympics. It even holds World Cups for beach soccer and futsal.

15
Number of tournaments FIFA runs.

- Soccer has many championship tournaments.
- Clubs compete to be named their countries' champions.
- The country champions then move on to the continent championship tournaments.
- National teams complete in the World Cup and other worldwide tournaments.

23

Everyone Loves the World Cup

Every four years, all eyes seem to be on soccer. The FIFA World Cup is the most watched sporting event in the world. Approximately 1 billion people watched the men's final of the 2014 World Cup between Germany and Argentina. That's close to one out of every seven people on the planet.

Each World Cup team features all-star players from their country.

For instance, Messi has played for Argentina. Ronaldo has played for Portugal. They were joined by other stars from their home countries. It doesn't matter which clubs the players play for professionally.

The road to the World Cup is long. More than 200 teams enter for a chance to play.

National teams gather from around the globe to compete for the World Cup trophy.

OTHER WORLD CUPS

The World Cup is so famous that other sports use the name for their championships. There is a World Cup in skiing. There's the World Cup of hockey. There's also a basketball World Cup.

Only 32 teams make the final tournament. It takes three years of play for a team to earn a spot at the World Cup. The tournament itself is also challenging. It lasts more than a month.

The World Cup is often the highlight of a player's career. Players such as Pelé became famous during the World Cup. In the 2015 World Cup Final, American Carli Lloyd became a household name. She scored three goals in the first 16 minutes of the championship game.

Carli Lloyd was a breakout star in the 2015 World Cup Final.

13
Countries that competed in the first World Cup in 1930.

- The World Cup is the biggest sporting event in the world.
- Teams play for three years to earn a spot in the World Cup.
- Players can become international heroes at the World Cup.

Soccer Has Memorable Moments

Soccer has many unforgettable moments. There have been amazing goals and saves. Some games are memorable from start to finish.

Just about everybody has a favorite moment. Pelé's first goal in the 1958 World Cup final is legendary. Even Pelé himself thought it was one of his best goals. Another favorite is Diego Maradona's second goal in the 1986 World Cup Final. Many fans consider it the best in the history of the tournament.

Few moments are as amazing as Brandi Chastain's winning penalty kick in the 1999 World Cup Final over China. The US women's team was under a lot of pressure to win the World Cup. They were the favored team. They were also playing in front of American fans. A scoreless tie forced a penalty kick

shootout. Chastain's penalty kick sealed the victory in thrilling style. The goal—and the entire game—is remembered as a historic moment in women's sports.

Sometimes failure is just as memorable as success. Fans may

90,185
Fans at the Rose Bowl stadium who watched Brandi Chastain's historic kick.

- Soccer has amazing moments with many favorites.
- Fans remember great goals from Pelé and Diego Maradona.
- Brandi Chastain's penalty kick and celebration were memorable.
- Sometimes mistakes in soccer are unforgettable, too.

never forget Roberto Baggio's missed penalty kick for Italy in the 1994 World Cup. Baggio had been a star throughout the tournament. But missing the penalty kick gave Brazil the victory.

Upsets have produced some great memories, too. The United States men beat England in the 1950 World Cup. North Korea stunned Italy in 1966. In each case, no one expected the underdog team to win.

Soccer fans will never forget Brandi Chastain's celebration after her winning penalty kick in 1999.

Fact Sheet

- One thing that shows soccer's popularity is an annual ranking of the world's most valuable sports teams. Since 2010, business magazine *Forbes* has ranked a soccer team number one in six out of the seven years. In 2016, Real Madrid, Manchester United, and FC Barcelona were three of the top five clubs. Real Madrid was estimated to be worth $3.65 billion.

- When Abby Wambach broke Mia Hamm's record for goals in international play in 2013, she broke it in style. Wambach came into the game against South Korea with 156 goals. Hamm's record was 158 goals. In the first 30 minutes, Wambach scored four goals.

- Penalty kick shootouts are a modern invention. In the past, when a tournament game was tied, extra time was played. If it was still tied, teams might flip a coin to determine the winner. Sometimes the entire game would be replayed several days or a week later. The first time a penalty shootout was used in a professional game was in 1970. The first time it was used at the World Cup was in 1982.

- The largest crowd to watch a soccer game was at the 1950 World Cup Final. Some estimates put the attendance as more than 200,000. Officially, 173,850 people paid to get into Rio de Janeiro's Maracana Stadium. It is the same stadium that was used for the 2014 World Cup Final and the 2016 Olympics. The stadium was renovated after the 1950 game to add more seats.

Glossary

amateur
Someone who participates in an activity without pay.

artificial
Made by humans; not natural.

endorsement
When someone publicly recommends a product or service.

foul
In soccer, an action the referee feels was unfair or illegal.

jersey
The shirt of a uniform.

knockout
A tournament format in which the loser of a game is eliminated, or knocked out, from the tournament.

penalty kick
A free kick on goal that is awarded after a certain type of foul or penalty is committed against a team.

stamina
The strength or power needed to complete a difficult task.

tifo
Any kind of large banner displayed at a game, usually by organized fan groups.

underdog
The team not expected to win.

upset
When the team favored to win loses to the underdog team.

For More Information

Books

Gifford, Clive. *Soccer.* Tarrytown, NY: Marshall Cavendish Benchmark, 2009.

Hurley, Michael. *Soccer.* Chicago: Heinemann-Raintree, 2013.

Marthaler, Jon. *Soccer Trivia.* Minneapolis: Abdo Publishing, 2016.

Visit 12StoryLibrary.com

Scan the code or use your school's login at **12StoryLibrary.com** for recent updates about this topic and a full digital version of this book. Enjoy free access to:

- Digital ebook
- Breaking news updates
- Live content feeds
- Videos, interactive maps, and graphics
- Additional web resources

Note to educators: Visit 12StoryLibrary.com/register to sign up for free premium website access. Enjoy live content plus a full digital version of every 12-Story Library book you own for every student at your school.

Index

About the Author

Brian Trusdell has been a sports writer for over 30 years. He has reported from six Olympics and four World Cups and has traveled to every continent except Antarctica. He lives in New Jersey with his wife.